DEDICATION

For every woman, who's ever suffered at the hands of a man who never deserved her love.

For my children, who should never have suffered and whose resilience and strength astounds me everyday.

For everyone who supported, understood and believed in us.

For anyone who still struggles to understand the complexities of abuse but is not afraid to try.

Survival

Gemma Bullivent

Presentation by *BookLeaf Publishing*

Web: www.bookleafpub.com

E-mail: info@bookleafpub.com

ISBN: 9789357745758

First edition 2023

PREFACE

A selection of poems about both abuse but more importantly about survival.

I'm Fine

I told someone "I'm fine" today,
Then someone asked again.
I nodded smiled and carried on,
I shouldn't burden them.

I told someone "I'm fine" today,
I pasted on the smile.
I didn't let them know the truth,
I've worn that mask a while.

I told someone "I'm fine" today,
The truth is just too hard.
My problems, no one else's,
I can't let down my guard.

I told someone "I'm fine" today,
Heart beating in my ears.
Anxiety it's taken hold,
No longer rational fears.

I told someone "I'm fine" today,
They knew it wasn't true.
There was a look of sympathy,
But there's nothing they can do.

I told someone "I'm fine" today,
The lie it felt too heavy.
Maybe I should open up,
I don't know if lm ready.

I told someone "I'm fine" today,
Words bitter on my tongue.
I knew l couldn't carry on,
The lie's been told too long.

I told someone "I'm fine" today,
They said they'd seen my cards.
I realised then what l would gain,
From letting down my guard.

I told someone "I'm fine" today,
Then stopped and said "I'm not".
I said l wasn't fine at all,
This life's become a lot.

I told someone "I'm fine" today,
It no longer felt a lie.
You only really start to live,
When you let the old life die.

The Narcassist

Their Empathy is lacking
Too Preoccupied with self
The strong erratic mood swings
Control, it is their wealth
With expectations unrealistic
Resulting self esteem is low
Don't dare to be their critic
Exaggeration, it's all a show
Obsession with appearance
Human qualities they hide
Approval's never left to chance
There's envy and there's pride
Until the day that you desist
Life in essence with the Narcissist

Farewell

You close your eyes to fall asleep,
In the hope it won't be there,
You close your eyes to drift someplace,
But the demons find you there.

You hope one day to discover,
That exit from your mind,
You hope that one day you'll forget,
The terror you left behind.

Somehow that battle gets harder,
New life just won't take hold,
The people that surround you,
Their ignorance is bold.

Bruises and cuts have healed now,
The swelling has long gone down,
The mental hell to hard to prove,
Too scared to make a sound.

Astonished after all the years,
When police won't investigate,
They asked him, they say he denied it,
All authorities claim it's too late.

There are victims that suffered before you,
They lived that identical hell,
Once again his abuse is not held to account,
A crime only worthy of farewell.

Why Never Again

I lie in the darkness
Wondering what l did wrong
I lie there alone
This has gone on to long

I can't touch him or kiss him
All affection is rare
He will flinch at my touch
There's no level of care

I swallow my tears
Crying silently too
Called pathetic, an annoyance
If that hurt should show through

l am always the problem
In his twisted mind
Always there for others
But to me just unkind

What wrong with you now?
The only response to my pain
It's not about me
I can't show it again

Just wanting connection
To him makes me strange
But he's shown it to others
Why never again?

Life to Renew

The anger deep within you,
When greater than the fear,
Can shatter the new life around you,
Not perfect, but you hold it so dear.

Your thoughts remain irrational,
The anxiety demands of you,
It takes away the logic,
The path that's your way through.

The pull to those who hurt you,
The magnet to trauma and despair,
You know the pain it causes,
But your heart still takes you there.

You crave a new beginning,
A life with someone new,
You know the path you need to take,
But your past, keeps haunting you.

You may escape the hell you lived,
Feel safe, away from harm,
But that comfort zone of terror,
Takes you back to kindred arms.

You want to find your knight,
To protect and value you.
You vow to keep on searching,
It's a dream, its your life to renew.

Abuse

Emotional abuse is a way to control
Another, using emotions and blame
To criticize, embarrass or otherwise
Manipulate another person and shame.

A consistent pattern of behaviours
Persistently destroy self belief
Undermining you, your mental health
There is no real chance of relief

Misunderstood, depressed, anxious,
You feel wounded, frustrated, confused,
Worthless, any time that you interact,
Chances high you are being used

Punish by withholding affection
The silent treatment so often given
Dissatisfied no matter how hard you try
New supply so often their ambition

Selfish, needy if you express thoughts
Dismiss your requests, wants, and needs
Behaviour erratic shortcomings not caught
The argument if you do not heed

Too sensitive, emotional, crazy
No longer permitted to feel
Consistently described as lazy
The exhaustion, all too real

Thankless

There is no thankless.
Love is giving your heart without expectation

They are thankless
They take your heart with expectation

My Stars

I know deep down you're scared,
Of the life you've had to face,
There's nothing left for you to fear,
Fear truly has no place.

You've done as much as you can do,
Worked hard with things so tough,
No one makes me quite as proud,
Don't ask me, it's always enough.

No matter what the outcome,
No matter the judgement you get,
You are an amazing shining star,
And life's hardly started yet.

Take your time and make your choice,
Do your best to keep your heart,
You know this all already,
Dont give up it's our new start.

When you finish all life's questions,
With lots of time to spare,
Just go back and check again,
I only say that cause l care.

There's only one competition,
That's with yourself, you'll see,
Remember no matter what the score,
You can always come to me.

Remember the past is not your smile,
Or the beauty of your soul,
Nor the reason we all love you,
The past doesn't make you whole.

I love you both my shining stars,
For all that you achieve,
No matter what life throws at us,
Your mum will never leave.

She said

I was damaged, broken, already abused didn't
want to take the chance. I nearly didn't but a
friend of his gave me hope….
"He'll always look after you" she said

He listened, understood, he wanted to help but I
questioned his motives. I'd seen it before but
I'd been told, why would she lie?
"He'll always look after you" she said

The anger took over just a flicker I saw
but I thought after everything I needed to not let
my past destroy a future…
"He'll always look after you" she said

The name calling, the mental abuse, the
escalation frightening us all but I needed to
remember the future could be bright….
"He'll always look after you" she said

Eventually having to call the police just to save
our family, what was left of our home she no
longer speaks to me as….
"He'll always look after you" she said

Survive

Someone asked me how I survived it
How I got past all the pain
How I found a way to face another day
How I found the strength to survive
I told them I haven't….
I'm still trying to find my own path after
walking his for so long.
I'm still in the dark but there's flickers of light I
can sometimes see.

I told them I haven't survived it
But every day I am surviving it

Stop

Stop asking why she doesn't leave
Start asking why she can't
Stop asking what she did so wrong
Start asking where's his heart

Stop saying what you would have done
Start saying what she can
Stop saying what you think is wrong
Start saying what's the plan

Stop doing what you think is right
Start doing what is asked
Stop doing what seems logical
Start doing what's forecast

Stop seeing what you want to see
Start seeing the life she lives
Stop seeing that it's easy
Start seeing what she gives

Life's Suitcase

She opens up life's suitcase,
And it's filled right to the top,
There just no longer is the space,
To fit more than her lot.

It's a bag filled of a lifetime,
Of the things she has lived through,
Been forgiven if she's thinking,
That there's nothing left to do.

But just because that bag is full,
Upon her face she paints a smile,
It does not mean it's easy,
The bag's been heavy for a while.

Her life it may look perfect,
But others can not say,
That the bag she has been carrying,
Is not a burden to her day.

She's walked though fire with monsters,
Pulled that bag along the way,
Been on the edge so many times,
The world thinking she's ok.

So never think it's light,
When she's dragged it all through hell,
Don't think her case's not heavy,
Because she carries it so well.

Change

You gave your soul to change them,
But that changed nothing.
You sacrificed friends and family,
Their lives remained the same.
You lost your pride and dignity,
While they seemed superior.
Your talents all diminished,
While their power is magnified.
Your focus to please them,
They're preoccupied with self
You focused on how you felt before,
Not how you are suffering now.

All you can change is yourself
But sometimes that changes everything

Forever

The Narcissistic keeps in contact,
To maintain their own control.
Don't want to give up power,
They won't release your soul.

Use children just to punish you,
Make you pay for leaving them.
It may be their fault you left,
But you're to blame once again.

Supply from your reaction,
They thrive off the "crazy" display.
No permission to move on with life,
They own you, you have to stay.

Keeping that close contact,
To hoover you back to the game.
Attempts to reason futile,
Forever, it will be the same.

Heeling

They lost control of you
You no longer protect them
You share your experiences
You're healing out loud
They use all they have left
Tell people you're crazy
You're an abuser
To turn people against you
To save face
You want to defend yourself
To clear your name
That only works against you
Believers were never on your side
Ignore it
Move on
Heel
Find happiness

Day by Day

That pain of abuse,
It never goes away,
You love and survive it,
Day by day.

Day by day,
It walks beside you,
That pain is real,
The battle is true.

The battle is true,
One day you wake,
Not knowing when,
They no longer take.

They no longer take,
As you no longer give,
But the hole it leaves,
You still have to live.

You still have to live,
Form a life from the start,
How do you do that,
When they broke your heart.

When they broke your heart,
With no ounce of care,
Them feeling nothing,
You're simply stripped bare.

You're simply stripped bare,
For their simple pleasure,
Nothing can heal you,
Joyful, not ever.

Joyful, not ever,
But there is always hope,
That one day you're able,
You're able to cope.

No One Gets Out Alive

They say don't take life to seriously,
No one gets out alive,
I didn't realise the truth of this,
Until the days l nearly died.

Death can be metaphorical,
Or literal, as you know,
But with those hands around your throat,
There is no place to go.

With death the way to leave this world,
It became a possible escape,
My soul had already died you see,
There's no hero, there's no cape.

Until that slow realisation,
That you have to save yourself,
To remove those hands around your throat,
You change the hand you're dealt.

Then one day those hands have gone
Fear of literal death abated
But you know that he still strangles you
That life of fear is fated

No Longer Broken

I felt stuck in the abuse,
My identity linked to experience, insecurity,
But I was not my traumas, my mistakes, my
past.
Pain, although part of my story,
Did not dictate my chapters to come.
With anger there was hope, sadness, care.
But once I was silent, my efforts exhausted
Your place in my life had gone
After the tears had dried, my vision and voice
became clear.
From the dark shadow there was light.
Finally finding myself.
Bruised, beautiful, bare
Stripped of my comforts but covered in truth.
Finally whole and healed.
No longer broken.

Milton Keynes UK
Ingram Content Group UK Ltd.
UKHW020644091023
430221UK00015B/681